Creative Content Development

Turning Ideas into an Income-Generating Business

Table of Contents

Chapter 1. Introduction

Liberate your imagination and step into the world of possibilities with our Special Report on "Creative Content Development: Turning Ideas into an Income-Generating Business". Seek inspiration within these pages as we navigate the thrilling byways of creativity and entrepreneurship. Whether you're a writer, designer, artist, or marketer, this report will nudge you past the precipice of hesitation into the thundering waterfall of your potential. Curated through extensive research and case studies, this report is designed to ignite your creative light, guide its transformation into a marketable product, and ultimately, fuel a sustainable business. Start your journey today and learn to convert your ideas into a source of income that not only satisfies your pocket but also kindles your passion!

Chapter 2. Discovering Your Creative Spark

Creativity is as ethereal as the whispers of wind through the trees, as fleeting as the glimmering embers of a dying fire. It is a vital force that can spring from the mundane routine, the echo of a conversation, or the depths of despair. Every individual possesses this divine spark; it wears different faces, manifests in varied forms, yet its fundamental essence remains the same. In the quest for understanding and empowering our creative energy, let's delve into the secrets of its discovery.

2.1. Unleashing the Power of Curiosity

The genesis of creative thinking often lies in the cradle of curiosity. Defined as a strong desire to learn or know something, curiosity has the potential to transform the barren plains of traditional thinking into a sprawling rainforest of innovative ideas.

The first step towards fostering curiosity involves embracing the unknown. It's about cultivating an openness towards fresh possibilities, diverse perspectives, and unprecedented avenues. As the renowned physicist Richard Feynman once stated, "I have no special talents, I am only passionately curious."

Begin by nurturing a questioning mind. Ask yourself why things are the way they are. Challenge norms. Encourage an insatiable appetite for learning that knows no satiation. Furthermore, incorporate curiosity into your everyday life. Engage with diverse fields of study. Embark on thought-provoking conversations. Read extensively, and most importantly, surround yourself with individuals who inspire curiosity within you.

2.2. Connecting Dots: Fostering Horizontal Thinking

The concept of horizontal thinking has recently gained popularity in the sphere of creativity. It revolves around drawing connections between seemingly unrelated domains – the ability to integrate various disciplines into a coherent whole.

To cultivate this knack for connecting dots, immerse yourself into diverse realms of knowledge. Gain insights from varied fields such as science, art, philosophy, literature, and more. When you expose your mind to different disciplines, it ignites a web of associations, resulting in unorthodox combinations that spark innovation.

Moreover, engage in multidisciplinary reading. This offers enriching perspectives that allow for brainstorming novel, unusual ideas. An engineer with an understanding of psychology or a marketer with an appreciation for art can yield unthinkable, progressive solutions. Thus, this multidisciplinary approach paves the way for boundless creation in your chosen field.

2.3. Embracing Chaos: The Role of Disorder in Creativity

Creativity often breeds in the thick of chaos. Unpredictability, uncertainty, and randomness may stir discomfort, yet they also serve as catalysts for groundbreaking ideas. An orderly mind, while efficient, may become confined within the boundaries of structure. Creativity, on the other hand, rebels against such constraints. It demands the freedom to wander, to explore unseen territories.

Begin by breaking free of rigid patterns. Allow room for flexibility, spontaneity, and improvisation. Embrace uncertainty and take calculated risks. Harness disorder as a springboard to leap into the domain of creative genius. Celebrate unconventional thinking, for it is the language of innovation.

2.4. Reigniting the Child Within

Children are distinguished by their abundant creativity, stemming loose from inhibitions, inhibitions being constructs fed to us as we mature. Learning to unlearn these constraints can stimulate extraordinary creative insights.

To reignite your inner child, be open to different experiences. View the world through a lens of fascination and wonder. Seek novelty, venture out of your comfort zone. Treat mistakes not as failures, but as stepping stones towards discovery. Remember, it is through exploration and experimentation that the most profound creative energy is unleashed.

2.5. Bringing it All Together: Nurturing Your Creative Spark

Having unearthed the keys to unlocking the creative spark, it's essential to cultivate a personal practice that fuels this flame. Here are a few strategies to nurture creative thinking:

- Develop routines that encourage creative exploration. Block time for undisturbed research, brainstorming, or ideation.

- Foster an environment that promotes open communication, constructive criticism, and free-flowing ideas.

- Regularly engage in creativity-stimulating activities, such as art, music, or innovative problem-solving.

- Make room for solitude. Being alone with your thoughts allows you to reflect on your experiences, draw connections, and generate new ideas.

- Keep a creative journal. It can serve as a repository for your thoughts, musings, and budding ideas.

Remember, nurturing your creative spark is an ongoing, rewarding process. It requires patience, resilience, and an unwavering faith in your capacity for creative transformation. By embracing curiosity, fostering horizontal thinking, accepting chaos, and reigniting the child within, you can navigate the labyrinth of creativity towards illuminating discoveries and inventive solutions.

Chapter 3. Turning Ideas Into Concrete Plans

Turning ideas into concrete plans is all about transforming your abstract thoughts and visions into actionable steps. It's about moving from dreaming to doing, from possibility to reality. This process entails several crucial stages, each of which will be considered in detail throughout this chapter. From understanding and evaluating your ideas, through setting goals and objectives, to creating a comprehensive action plan — this journey will guide you step by step to make your aspiration a tangible venture.

3.1. Understanding and Evaluating Your Idea

The first place to start is with the idea itself. For an idea to become a concrete plan, you need to have a thorough understanding and evaluation of its market relevancy and feasibility.

To do so, become what we call an "informed judge" of your own ideas. Gather as much data as possible. Look into trends, the performance of similar ideas, and current market gaps. Combine this with your knowledge and expertise to assess the viability of your idea.

Consider using SWOT analysis – a tool that helps understand the Strengths, Weaknesses, Opportunities and Threats related to the business. This technique could assist in carving out a sustainable niche in your market.

An idea might be brilliant but it's only as good as its execution. Ensure you have the skills, resources, and passion required to turn that idea into a reality.

3.2. Setting Goals and Objectives

Now that you've deeply evaluated your idea, it's time to set goals. As the old saying goes, "A goal without a plan is just a wish." Goals are critical in turning abstract ideas into concrete realities.

Start with a clear vision of what you want to achieve. Be specific, measurable, attainable, relevant and time-bound. These SMART goals act as the backbone of your business plan.

Set both long and short-term objectives. The long-term goals will guide your vision while the short-term ones act as milestones leading to the final destination.

Always bear in mind, these goals should align with your overall business objectives and vision.

3.3. Creating a Comprehensive Action Plan

After setting your goals, it's time to create a comprehensive strategy and action plan. This step-by-step guide will serve as your road map in your journey to convert your ideas into a sustainable business.

Identifying steps: Break down all activities you need to perform to achieve your goals. These should include finance planning, marketing strategies, resources needed, among others.

Sequence: Arrange these steps in a logical, effective order. Which should be first? Which follows after? Each task depends on the completion of the one before it. Tailor these sequences to your specific business needs.

Responsibilities: Assign tasks to specific persons or teams in your business. This division of labor can greatly enhance productivity and efficiency.

Timeline: Set a realistic timeline for each task. Consider the dependencies of each step and factor in sufficient cushion time for unforeseen delays.

3.4. Monitoring and Reviewing Your Plan

Once your action plan is in place, it's crucial to frequently monitor and review it. This helps gauge progress, test the effectiveness of your plan, and make timely revisions.

Review the plan's progress against your set timelines. Evaluate whether every step is contributing to their respective goals. Use this data to track what's working and what isn't.

Based on your observations, adjust your plan accordingly. Adapt, learn, and grow. Turning ideas into concrete plans isn't a one-time activity but rather a dynamic, evolving journey.

Turning ideas into concrete plans can seem like a colossal task. However, with a systematic approach, you can guide your ideas from mere possibilities to tangible realities. Understand your idea, set clear goals, develop a comprehensive action plan, and review your progress. Embrace the process, learn from each step, and soon, you can watch your idea grow into a thriving, income-generating venture.

Chapter 4. Structuring Your Creative Business Model

In a truly creative venture, your business model is as unique and expressive as the goods or services you provide. With that in mind, understanding the mechanics of a business model is still crucial because it provides structure and direction. Careful structuring of your model will ensure that your ideas translate into an income-generating machine, feeding not just your bank account but also your passion.

4.1. Identifying Your Unique Value Proposition

The heartbeat of your creative business model is your Unique Value Proposition (UVP). This crystallizes what makes you stand out amidst a sea of competition. Reflect and identify what makes your creative outputs unique. It could be your style, your messaging, or the medium of your creativity. For writers, it could be the way you spin a story. For artists, it could be your stylistic brush strokes or your choice of canvas.

This unique proposition is what makes customers choose your products or services over others. It can lead to customers being willing to pay a higher premium or build a loyal following for your work. Remember, value isn't necessarily what you put into the service, it's what users derive out of it.

4.2. Understanding Your Customer Segments

Identifying your customer segments is pivotal in structuring your business model. Who are you creating for? Who finds value in what you sell? Understanding your audience helps you tailor your creative content to their wants and needs. This includes demographics like age, education, or geographical location, as well as psychographics such as interests, behaviors, or lifestyles.

Remember that in a creative business, it's not always about selling to the masses. You can create a niche product for a specific audience and still generate viable income. Catering to the unique preferences of a smaller market can often generate much higher value.

4.3. Streamlining Distribution Channels

Distribution channels are the roads that connect your creative content with customers. How and where will you provide your service or product? Will it be online through an e-commerce platform or physical outlets like an art gallery or store? Understand that each distribution channel comes with its own pros and cons. For instance, a physical gallery gives customers the opportunity to view your work in person, but limits access to only those in the vicinity. E-commerce can reach out to a vast audience internationally but takes away the tangible experience of viewing or feeling the product.

You also have to analyze your audience's preferences. Where do they usually shop? Do they prefer having products delivered to them or do they like to go to a physical store? Knowing this can significantly increase your chances of successful transactions.

4.4. Structuring Revenue Streams

Depending on the nature of your product or service, there are numerous ways to generate income. You can sell your products at a set price, or you can offer them on a subscription basis. You can also explore hosting paid workshops or licensing your creative content. Explore different revenue models and identify which can bring you the most income while preserving the integrity of your creative work.

4.5. Establishing Key Partnerships

In a creative business, collaborations can lead to expanded customer reach and increased resources. It might be beneficial to form alliances with other individuals or organizations that can provide related services to your clientele. For instance, if you're a painter, you might want to partner with an art supply store or a picture framing service. If you're a designer, printers or fabric suppliers could be potential partners. Partnerships do not have to be formal; even informal arrangements can pave the way for mutual benefits.

4.6. Cost Structure

The cost structure enlists all the financial resources you need to operate your business. This includes both your fixed and variable costs. Fixed costs are those that do not change regardless of how much you produce, like rent and salaries. Variable costs fluctuate with your production volume like raw materials or shipping costs. Understanding your cost structure can help you price your creative pieces appropriately and make profitable decisions.

Not every creative business model looks the same, they can be as diverse and unique as the art they generate. However, by analyzing these core components, you can form a structured, comprehensive plan to guide your creation from idea to income. Remember, your business model is like your canvas - it's up to you to paint your path to success.

Chapter 5. The Art of Storytelling in Content Development

In the world of creative content development, storytelling is an irreplaceable asset and a potent skill. As simple as it may seem, it is genuinely an art with intimately woven complexities and nuances that require honing and mastering.

5.1. Understanding Storytelling

Whether it's a tale told around a campfire, a novel, or content for a marketing campaign, a story is a compelling way to convey information and engage an audience. It's not solely about telling tales; it's about how you present information, how you make it appealing, and how you bring it to life.

Storytelling is an art that depends upon your ability to intrigue your audience with a narrative, stimulate their curiosity, evoke their emotions, and touch upon their intellects. It is about tying together the strings of words, images, sounds, and emotions into a coherent and immersive entity.

In the context of content development, storytelling becomes the light that illuminates the path you want your audience to tread. Be it a promotion, a social cause, an element of education, or an eye-opening perspective – when you wrap your content around an engaging story, your audience is more likely to relate to it and consequently respond to your call-to-action.

5.2. Elements of a Story

Understanding how to weave a riveting story entails recognizing the structure and elements that make up a narrative. While the specifics can vary, there are general components that stories share.

- Setting: This is where and when the story occurs, providing a backdrop against which the action takes place.

- Characters: The people or beings in the story. Creating memorable characters is crucial to establishing a connection with your audience.

- Plot: This is the sequence of events that form the body of the story. The plot organizes the characters' actions and choices, and their outcomes.

- Conflict: This refers to the challenges or obstacles the characters must overcome. Conflict is the driving force of the plot.

- Resolution: This is how the conflict is resolved. It's also the ending of the story.

Knowing these elements, and effectively employing them, is important in engaging your audience with your content.

5.3. Storytelling Techniques

While understanding the basic elements of a story is crucial, the magic truly unfurls when we delve into the specifics of storytelling techniques. These techniques help in shaping your content, making it resonant and impactful.

5.3.1. Show, Don't Tell

One of the most potent techniques in storytelling is to "show, don't tell". This concept highlights the importance of letting the audience explore the details for themselves rather than spoon-feeding them each morsel of data. Let's say you're crafting a narrative about a character overcoming adversity. Instead of merely stating "Jane was brave", opt for "Jane trembled at the sound of the booming thunder but didn't flinch. She took a deep breath, held it in, and stepped into the maelstrom."

5.3.2. Creating Engaging Characters

Characters are the soul of your story, and extensive effort should be invested not just in describing them but also in developing their characteristics and persona. Are they audacious or timid? Are they rational or emotional? By illustrating your characters' qualities thoroughly, you bring them to life and enable your audience to form connections with them.

Indeed, storytelling is not a mere course of telling events as they transpired; it is about employing various techniques to make it immersive and engaging.

5.4. The Power of Storytelling in Content Development

Storytelling possesses a unique power to connect where plain information often fails. It adds context, evokes emotions and ultimately ingrains your message deeper in the minds of your audience. It immerses your audience in a journey, it carries them along through different emotions, evoking empathy and ultimately leading them to identify with the story. This identification brings about a subsequent impact on their behaviors and actions. In terms of content development, this is precisely what you would want your content to achieve.

In a sea of countless content providers, consumers have an endless array of options. Storytelling makes your content stand out, making it memorable and engaging. It allows you to go beyond the simple process of presenting information and enable you to forge a connection with your audience, making content marketing far more effective.

In conclusion, storytelling is an indispensable tool in the armory of any content developer. Regardless of whether your content involves narrative-driven campaigns or data-driven reports, the possession and fluxing of this storytelling skill will enable you to create more engaging, more meaningful, and ultimately more effective content. Mastering the art of storytelling, therefore, is fundamental to turning your ideas into an income-generating business.

Chapter 6. Harnessing Technology for Creative Content

In the old days, artists and creators used traditional mediums such as paint, pencils, and paper to express their visions, whereas writers, marketers, and other professionals required physical venues or tangible materials to reach their audience. Yet, in this era of digitalization, technology is our friend and means of simplification. Through harnessing the power of technology, creators can convert raw ideas into high-value content that not only attracts an audience but also generates profits if effectively commercialized.

6.1. Harnessing Social Media & Online Platforms

If you're in the creative industry today, the internet is your showcase, and social media is your ticket to worldwide exposure. Platforms like Instagram, TikTok, YouTube, Twitter, and the more professionally oriented LinkedIn provide an incredible toolset for content creators. Whether you're a photographer looking to showcase your portfolio, a writer looking to blog and generate followers, or a marketer looking to reach a wider audience, these platforms can propel your brand to previously unimagined heights.

Beyond mere exposure, social media also provides analytics tools that can provide insights. These tools can assist in understanding audience behavior and preferences better. Such information is exceptionally important to refine your content and make it more attractive, shareable, and hence, profitable.

6.2. Integration of Design Tools and Software

In creative content development, having artistic talent or a knack for storytelling is not enough. One must master the right tools and software, like Adobe Premiere Pro for video editing or Adobe Photoshop for graphic design. These tools can help you transform your raw ideas into aesthetically pleasing and engaging final products.

If you're into writing or copywriting, tools like Grammarly and Hemingway can greatly help improve your language, clarity and aid in error checking. Similarly, SEO tools like SEMRush and Google Trends help content creators optimize the visibility of their content on search engines, thereby increasing the potential for organic traffic and income.

6.3. Adopting E-commerce for Monetization

As a content creator, it's essential to consider your monetization platforms right from the start. Besides earning through advertising and sponsored content - which often requires you have significant viewership, other direct income-generation options are possible thanks to e-commerce.

Today, there are several e-commerce platforms such as Etsy and Redbubble for artists and creatives who create physical products. Digital products such as photos, ebooks, or online courses, can be sold on platforms like Gumroad or Teachable.

6.4. Leverage on Learning, Skill Development Platforms

Technologies like high-speed internet and online learning platforms have made upskilling and reskilling easier than ever. Platforms like Coursera, Udacity, or Skillshare have thousands of courses for creatives. These courses impart knowledge about various tools, content development techniques, SEO strategies, and other relevant topics. Meanwhile, websites like GitHub or StackOverflow offer learning resources for those interested in the technology behind websites and apps.

6.5. Embracing the Power of Data

In the current market, data is the new electricity. Information about consumer behavior, interests, and buying patterns can give you significant leverage over competitors. Using tools like Google Analytics or similar digital analytics software can help you collect and analyze this data to create more targeted and valuable content.

As we move forward, technology will continue to open up new avenues for creative content development. Navigating this landscape may feel daunting at first, but with the right knowledge and tools, it can become an exhilarating journey. Remember, technology is a tool that works best when it serves us and our creative energy - not when it overwhelms us. Harnessing its power effectively and sagaciously is key to turning ideas into a compelling and profitable creative business.

Chapter 7. Intellectual Property: Protecting Your Ideas

Starting your entrepreneurial journey may be filled with an abundance of enthusiasm and drive, but to secure your business success, it's essential to protect the life source of your enterprise: your creative ideas. This investment could spell the difference between navigating through innovation-rich waters or stranded and bereft in an intellectual wilderness. Let's discuss how you can protect your intellectual property crucial for sustainable creative content development.

7.1. Understanding Intellectual Property

Before we delve into the protection of your intellectual property (IP), it's crucial to first understand what it is. Intellectual property refers to creations of the mind, such as literary works, inventions, designs, symbols, images, and names used in commerce. These can inherently possess either aesthetic or commercial value.

IP is safeguarded through specific rights that are categorized into four main types: copyright, trademark, patent, and trade secret. Understanding the differences between these rights would allow you to choose the correct one, ensuring comprehensive protection for your creations.

7.2. Copyright: Shield for Your Creativity

Copyright represents an exclusive set of rights granted to the creator of an original work. These rights include the opportunity to reproduce the work, to create derivative works, to distribute copies, and to perform or display the work publicly.

Whether you are an author penning your novel or a graphic designer morphing concepts into eye-catching visual narratives, the assurance of copyright protection enables you to control how your work is reproduced, distributed, and presented before the public eye. Remember, your works are automatically protected by copyright once they are created and fixed in a tangible form.

7.3. Trademarks: Protecting Your Brand Identity

A trademark is a recognizable insignia, phrase, word, or symbol that denotes a specific product and legally differentiates it from all other products of its kind. A trademark exclusively associates a product with a particular brand.

An integral part of creative content development is creating a unique brand identity. A strong, identifiable trademark, as simple as a logo or a business name, serves as the touchpoint for your brand's identity in the market, helping customers distinguish your services or products from others. Registering your trademark ensures your brand's authenticity and keeps impostors at bay.

7.4. Patents: Safeguarding Your Inventions

A patent is an exclusive right granted to an inventor for an innovative product or a newly improved process. It prevents others from creating, using, selling, or importing the patented invention, offering a protective barrier of up to 20 years.

Content developers involved in devising unique apps or technology platforms for delivering content should leverage the strength of patents. It allows for competitive advantage while preserving the originality of their invention.

7.5. Trade Secrets: Valuable Business Information Stealth

Trade secrets encompass any confidential business information which provides an enterprise a competitive edge. It includes manufacturing or industrial secrets and commercial secrets. The unauthorized use of such information by persons other than the holder is regarded as an unfair practice and a violation of the trade secret.

Unique insights into market trends, unpublished content, exclusive methods of content creation or optimization, and undisclosed marketing strategies can all be protected under the umbrella of trade secrets. Unlike other IP rights, a trade secret can potentially last forever, provided the information remains confidential.

7.6. Register and Enforce Your Intellectual Property Rights

Knowing about intellectual property rights is not enough; it's crucial to register and enforce them appropriately. Engage a patent attorney, approach the copyright office, or contact your national trademark institution for registration procedures. An unregistered IP right is an unprotected one.

However, the end doesn't stop at registration. Remember that protection is not defensible unless enforced. Keep an eye out for possible infringement cases and have the legal means ready to protect your IP when necessary.

7.7. How to Leverage Your Intellectual Property

Your secured IP is not just a badge of protection; it can be a source of income too. Licensing, franchising, and selling your copyright, patents, trademarks, or trade secrets, can generate monetary gains and create multiple profit avenues for your enterprise.

Creative content development is a rich, innovative journey that sows the seeds of extraordinary ideas. To ensure your creations confer the desired profit and recognition, they deserve the essential protection of intellectual property rights. Remember, a secured idea is not only a barrier against potential infringement but also a bridge to endless business opportunities. By safeguarding your novel ideas today, you are investing in your bountiful long-term success and viability. Let your ideas flow with courage and confidence, knowing that they are embraced by the secure arms of intellectual property rights.

Chapter 8. Marketing Your Creative Content: Strategies for Success

Once you've honed your craft and created compelling content, it's time to share your masterpiece with the world. But how do you transform from creator to entrepreneur? Effective marketing strategies are vital to ensure your creative project doesn't go unnoticed. In this chapter, we shall discuss the strategies that can help your creative content shine.

8.1. Understanding Your Audience

As with any business venture, understanding your audience is key. Take the time to research who is likely to enjoy your content – both in terms of demographic factors like age, location, and occupation, and psychographic factors like interests and lifestyle. With these insights, you can shape your content and marketing strategies to attract and engage your target audience.

Make use of data analytics tools, conduct surveys, or leverage social media to gather information. Remember that understanding your audience is a continuous loop of learning, adapting, creating, and, in turn, learning again.

8.2. Building Your Brand

Your brand is more than just a logo or a catchy slogan; it's the promise of your unique value that sets you apart from others. Defining your brand identity requires introspection, creativity, and a crystal-clear understanding of your unique selling proposition (USP).

Work on your logo, website, color palette, and tone of voice. Curate a brand personality that speaks directly to your audience. Any form of communication, be it a social media post or a formal email, should reflect your brand's personality and tone.

8.3. Crafting a Compelling Story

Powerful stories captivate audiences and providers consumers with a pathway to connect with your brand on an emotional level. Whether you're selling a product, a service, or a cause, narratives woven into your content can stimulate empathy, engagement, and action.

Speak about your vision, mission, and the journey you've embarked upon to reach here. Unravel how your love for your craft motivated you to share it with the world. Be transparent and genuine – remember, authentic stories resonate most.

8.4. Using Social Media Strategically

Social media can act as a powerful amplifier for your creative content. Utilizing these platforms effectively requires planning and strategizing, from choosing the right platforms to creating engaging content and building community engagement.

Tailor your content for each platform. For Instagram, use visually captivating images or short videos. On Twitter, use short, punchy phrases to succinctly express your message. LinkedIn works well for professional or industry-specific content while Facebook is a versatile platform suited to a range of content types.

Don't underestimate the power of hashtags. They help categorize your content and increase its visibility. Also, engage with the comments on your posts, maintain conversations, and build relationships.

8.5. Implementing SEO

Search engine optimization (SEO) is a process you undertake to increase your content visibility on search engines. Understand and use relevant keywords, optimize your website's loading speed, employ high-quality images, create internal links, and ensure mobile optimization.

Online tools like Google Keyword Planner or SEMRush can help you find the most relevant keywords. Remember, SEO is a continuous process, and staying updated with the latest practices is crucial for your visibility online.

8.6. Email Marketing

Despite the growth of social media, email continues to be a potent tool for digital marketing. It offers you a direct line of communication with your audience. From newsletters to promotional offers, use email to keep subscribers engaged and informed about your latest content.

Ensure to grow your email list organically through lead magnets or subscription forms on your website. Prioritize quality over quantity; it's better to have a list of genuinely interested subscribers rather than a huge, disinterested list.

8.7. Hosting Webinars or Workshops

Offer value before asking for commitment. Hosting webinars or workshops centered around the knowledge or skills you bring to the table can attract potential customers. You can use these opportunities to showcase your expertise, engage with your audience, and later on, gently introduce your product or service.

8.8. Collaborating with Influencers

Influencer marketing presents a rich vein of engagement and exposure. Partner with influencers whose values align with your brand and who have an audience that matches your target in demographics and interests. This can open up your content to new audiences and potentially generate more interest.

8.9. Personalizing Your Marketing

In an age of information overload, personalized marketing can help you stand out. Personalization can take various forms – from addressing an email recipient by name to offering content or product recommendations based on past behavior. Such strategies make your audience feel valued, boosting engagement and conversions.

Your journey from crafting creative content to marketing it effectively can be an adventurous one. It requires strategic planning, incessant learning, genuine connection with your audience, and an undying passion for your craft. Remember, success doesn't usually come overnight, and persistence goes a long way. Stay focused on your passion, embrace the evolution of your brand, and continually seek innovation in your marketing strategies. You are on your way to paving your path as an entrepreneur with creative content.

Chapter 9. Networking and Building Strategic Partnerships

Networking and forming strategic partnerships is one of the foundational elements of a successful venture. This process involves connecting with others in your industry or relevant sectors, creating symbiotic relationships that support your business's growth and acceleration.

9.1. Understanding The Importance of Networking

Networking is more than just swapping contact information at an industry event. It's also about establishing and fostering relationships that can provide mutual benefit. Networking allows businesses to connect with each other, share ideas, and collaborate on projects. It may lead to gaining new clients, partnerships, or even mergers and acquisitions.

Networking opens doors to conversations that would not occur otherwise, encouraging collaborative thinking and the sharing of insights from different perspectives. A simple introduction or conversation can spark fresh ideas, create partnerships, or even save your company from pursuing an ill-advised path.

9.2. The Art of Networking

The first step in successful networking is understanding that it is an exchange of value. Before diving into it, consider what you can offer others, such as your knowledge, resources, or connections.

Start by identifying your potential networking sphere. It includes your existing connections, industry professionals, suppliers, influencers in your field, or even potential customers. Don't limit yourself to your industry, think outside the box. Someone in an unrelated field might offer insights that could revolutionize your approach.

Next, establish communication. Reach out to these individuals or organizations, introducing yourself, and your business. Be sure to communicate the unique value you bring, and express an interest in learning about the individual or organization you're reaching out to. Remember to be genuine, as people appreciate authenticity.

Always follow up on your interactions. Sending a note of thanks, a relevant article, or sharing opportunities keeps the communication line open. Building relationships takes time and consistency.

9.3. Creating Strategic Partnerships

Strategic partnerships occur when two or more businesses align for a set period, to achieve mutual goals. These partnerships can take various forms, such as marketing partnerships, joint ventures, licensing agreements, or even affiliate partnerships.

The first step in creating a strategic partnership is identifying potential partners. Assess businesses that complement yours or share similar goals, and consider how you could create mutually beneficial opportunities. For example, a graphic designer and a content writer could form a partnership, providing clients with a comprehensive content creation package.

Forming a strategic partnership requires negotiation and defining common ground. Both parties need to collaboratively draft a partnership proposal, detailing responsibilities, shared tasks, and how benefits would be proportionally distributed.

9.4. Managing Networking and Partnerships

Managing your network, and any partnerships you form, requires frequent maintenance and follow-ups. Regularly check in with your contacts and partners, update them on your business, ask about their progress, and explore areas for collaboration.

Networking and partnering demand a level of tact and diplomacy, as you'll navigate differing opinions and interests. Cultivate good listening skills, remain open to feedback, and address any issues promptly and professionally.

Remember, the goal is to foster long-lasting relationships that benefit all parties involved. Set clear expectations, establish trust, and be willing to contribute as much as you gain.

9.5. Tools and Resources for Networking

There are numerous tools available to assist you in networking and partnership building. Social media platforms like LinkedIn, Twitter, or industry-specific networking sites are a great start. Conferences and industry events also provide networking opportunities.

Networking tools like contact management software can help you organize and track your contacts and interactions. Also, collaboration tools like Slack, Skype, or Trello can facilitate communication and project management within partnerships.

In conclusion, networking and building strategic partnerships is a multi-faceted process. It demands effort, consistency, and continued nurturing. But, the benefits it brings not only enhances your business's growth prospects, but also cultivates a supportive and innovative entrepreneurial ecosystem around you.

Chapter 10. Managing Financial Aspects of Your Content Business

Whether you're just starting on the journey to monetize your creative works or seeking to optimize the business aspect of your current content creation, it's important to understand the financial dynamics that not only sustain but also help scale your endeavors.

To make your passion profitable, you need to be well-versed not only in content creation but also in financial management. Understanding the importance of budgeting, financial tracking, and revenue diversification is fundamental to ensuring the financial health and scalability of your content business. Achieving this understanding will inform your daily decisions and long-term strategies, making you a disciplined business owner who willingly embraces both creativity and pragmatism.

10.1. Creating a Budget for Your Content Business

Creating a budget can feel daunting, especially when you're in the early stages of your business. Your income might fluctuate from month to month, and expenses may seem vague or unexpected. Despite these uncertainties, having a budget is crucial to predict and track income and to control spending.

Your budget can be either 'top-down' or 'bottom-up'. A 'top-down' budget means you define the amount you wish to spend and allocate it to different categories. With a 'bottom-up' budget, you identify all the costs you will incur and total them to get the amount needed. There isn't a single approach that fits all. The method you choose should align with your thinking and financial planning ability.

One key to budgeting is to overestimate expenses and underestimate income. This conservative approach can safeguard against unexpected costs and drops in income, ensuring more sustainability for your content business.

10.2. Financial Tracking and Analysis

Keeping track of your financials is an ongoing task that aids in predicting trends and preventing issues. A well-maintained and analyzed financial record can paint a clear picture of where your business stands, where it is heading, and what needs mitigating or capitalizing upon.

Understanding your revenue streams, tracking your income, and of course, knowing your costs is fundamental. Invest in a good accounting software which offers robust features such as invoicing, tax calculation, expense tracking, and comprehensive reporting.

Remember, scrutinizing these numbers isn't only a year-end task. The more frequently you assess, the easier it is to spot trends and make adjustments. This regular evaluation can pave the way to prosperous financial health.

10.3. Understanding Your Revenue Distribution and Diversification

Recognize that a single revenue source may not be sustainable long-term. Revenue diversification can help mitigate the instability often associated with content business. Selling your content through various channels, building a loyal subscriber base, offering premium or exclusive content, and diversifying into associated products or services can all serve as buffers against irregular income.

Investigate your revenue distribution - where are most of your profits coming from? Which channels are underperforming? A precise analysis of your distribution strategy can lead to valuable pivots and growth.

10.4. Pricing Your Content

Pricing your content appropriately is crucial. You should account not only for your time and resources but also for your creative talent. This might mean valuing your work higher than what a strictly time-and-materials approach would suggest.

In order to price your content accurately, investigate your industry norms, analyze competitor pricing strategies, and consider your audience's paying capacity. Being clear about your pricing model - be it subscription-based, one-time purchase, or donation-based - can also help you create effective marketing strategies.

10.5. Planning for Financial Growth

Like every business, the end goal for your content business should also be to grow. Having a financial growth plan helps in mapping out how you want your earnings to increase over time, and what strategies and resources you will employ for the same.

Tying it all together, managing the financial aspects of your content business, although a meticulous task, is a key determinant of your overall success. Make it a continuous learning process, and don't be afraid of making mistakes. They are often stepping stones leading to smart strategies and sustainable growth. The more disciplined you become in maintaining financial health, the more fulfilling your journey as a content entrepreneur will be.

Chapter 11. Ensuring Sustainability and Growth in the Creative Economy

The sustainability of a creative business is not just about making sure there is enough profit for ongoing expenses and operations. It is about creating an ecosystem that will inspire constant creativity, attract loyal customers, foster a nourishing environment for employees, and establish a strong brand that stands the test of time. Let us delve into how you can ensure sustained growth and prosperity in your creative economy venture.

11.1. Developing Your Niche

In the world of creative content development, knowing your niche and understanding it comprehensively is pivotal to sustainability. This not only includes a deep comprehension of your art form or medium but equally involves a nuanced awareness of your target audience and their needs.

Understanding your niche gives your business a sense of direction and purpose, ensuring all efforts and strategies are focused towards serving it effectively. Your niche will help you develop a distinct brand voice which will make your product stand out amidst numerous competitors. It puts your business on the path of outshining generic brands by being specialist content creators who appeal to a very specific audience segment.

11.2. Diversifying Your Content

While your niche is pivotal for your brand identity, it is equally important to incorporate diversity in the content you create. This provides an opportunity to grab a broader customer base while it keeps your offering fresh and appealing.

Content could be diversified by experimenting with various genres, layouts, designs, or themes. Varied collaborations with diverse artists or brands can also breathe new life into content. The aim should be crafting a well-curated mix of consistent, high-quality content that appeals to a broad spectrum of tastes within your niche. This ensures your relevance in the ever-evolving marketplace and captures a broader set of potential customers.

11.3. Streamlining Marketing Strategies

Marketing strategies act as the vessels which deliver your crafted content to the right audience at the right time. Success in the creative economy often hinges on whether your potential audience is aware of your presence. Hence, marketing needs to be dynamic, adaptable, and always evolving.

With the digital era ushering in varied platforms, formats, and ways to interact with consumers, it is essential to keep updating your marketing strategies involving social media marketing, influencer collaborations, affiliate marketing, content marketing, and SEO. It's essential to analyse and understand which platform serves your needs the best and focus your efforts accordingly.

11.4. Embracing Innovation

Being versatile and open to innovation is a key determinant of sustainability within the creative economy. The innovation may come in varied forms, from incorporating new technologies to adopting unique production processes, or even crowd-sourcing content from your audience.

Continuous innovation ensures you remain relevant and competitive, as the creative space is continually evolving. This ensures longevity and sustainability, as you're constantly on the forefront of change, catering to the evolving needs of your audience.

11.5. Building Community Engagement

Sustainability in the creative economy can often hinge on the strength of the community you build around your business. Engagement and interaction with your community can cultivate a loyal customer base who actively advocate for your brand.

Consider developing strategies that invite interaction, such as feedback sessions, community events, or social media engagement. Valuing your customers' opinions fosters a strong sense of belonging and co-creation. This will not only provide you with invaluable insights into what your customers want but also present opportunities for co-creation, establishing a sense of ownership among your audience.

11.6. Establishing Strong Financial Planning

Strong financial planning underpins every sustainable business. Creative ventures often face financial challenges since most income streams in this field are uncertain and unpredictable. Therefore, meticulous forecasting of revenues and costs, prudent management of funds, looking out for diverse income streams, and having a solid backup plan for financial crunches form the bedrock of a sustainable creative business.

11.7. Nurturing Your Creative Soul

Sustainability and growth in a creative economy don't just stop at ensuring the business is stable. It is about making sure you are continuously nourished as well. A creative enterprise thrives on your creativity, which needs regular nurturing.

Spending time working on personal projects, taking creative breaks, engaging in activities for personal growth and enrichment, going for creative bootcamps or retreats, and reading up on inspirations are just a few ways to keep the creative juices flowing.

Embedding such practices into your business model can ensure that not only your business but also your creativity sustain and grow over time. This ensures the prosperity of your unique voice, a sense of authenticity in your work, which can push the boundaries of success, making your business a creative powerhouse.

Indeed, sustainability in the creative economy offers a challenging yet rewarding journey. Embrace your unique voice, practice resilience, involve your community, and never stop learning. Herein lies the secret of ensuring sustainability and growth in the creative economy.